Wendell Berry
TRAVELING

COUNTERPOINT
BERKELEY

AT HOME

Wood Engravings by John DePol

"A Walk Down Camp Branch" is reprinted from *Recollected Essays,* copyright © 1981 by Wendell Berry.

The poems "Traveling at Home," "The Winter Rain," "Winter Night Poem for Mary," "Meditation in the Spring Rain," "History," "Woods," "The Lilies," "Another Descent," "Creation Myth," and "In Rain" are reprinted from *Collected Poems 1957– 1982,* copyright © 1985 by Wendell Berry.

The poems "The Bell Calls in the Town," "The Eager Dog Lies Strange and Still," "Thrush Song, Stream Song, Holy Love," "The Year Relents," "A Tired Man Leaves His Labor" are excerpted from *Sabbaths,* copyright © 1987 by Wendell Berry.

LIBRARY OF CONGRESS CATALOGING-IN-PUBLICATION DATA

Berry, Wendell, 1934–
  Traveling at home / Wendell Berry.
    p. cm.
  ISBN 978-1-58243-764-4
  I. Title.
  PS3552.E75T7 1989   89-32376
  811'.54—dc20   CIP

COUNTERPOINT
1919 Fifth Avenue
Berkeley, CA 94710

www.counterpointpress.com
Distributed by Publishers Group West
Printed in Canada

10 9 8 7 6 5 4 3 2 1

CONTENTS

TRAVELING AT HOME

SECTION ONE

A Walk Down Camp Branch

I start down from one of the heights of the upland, the town of Port Royal at my back. It is a winter day, overcast and still, and the town is closed in itself, humming and muttering a little, like a winter beehive.

The dog runs ahead, prancing and looking back, knowing the way we are about to go. This is a walk well established with us—a route in our minds as well as on the ground. There is a sort of mystery in the establishment of these ways. Any time one crosses a given stretch of country with some frequency, no matter how wanderingly one begins, the tendency is always toward habit. By the third or fourth trip, without realizing it, one is following a fixed path, going the way one went before. After that, one may still wander, but only by deliberation, and when there is reason to hurry, or when the mind wanders rather than the feet, one returns to the old route. Familiarity has begun. One has made a relationship with the landscape, and

11

the form and the symbol and the enactment of the relationship is the path. These paths of mine are seldom worn on the ground. They are habits of mind, directions and turns. They are as personal as old shoes. My feet are comfortable in them.

From the height I can see far out over the country, the long open ridges of the farmland, the wooded notches of the streams, the valley of the river opening beyond, and then more ridges and hollows of the same kind.

Underlying this country, nine hundred feet below the highest ridgetops, more than four hundred feet below the surface of the river, is sea level. We seldom think of it here; we are a long way from the coast, and the sea is alien to us. And yet the attraction of sea level dwells in this country as an ideal dwells in a man's mind. All our rains go in search of it and, departing, they have carved the land in a shape that is fluent and falling. The streams branch like vines, and between the branches the land rises steeply and then rounds and gentles into the long narrowing fingers of ridgeland. Near the heads of the streams even the steepest land was not too long ago farmed and kept cleared. But now it has been given up and the woods is returning. The wild is flowing back like a tide. The arable ridgetops reach out above the gathered trees like headlands into the sea, bearing their human burdens of fences and houses and barns, crops and roads.

Looking out over the country, one gets a sense of the whole of it: the ridges and hollows, the clustered buildings of the farms, the open fields, the woods, the stock ponds set like coins into the slopes. But this is a surface sense, an exterior sense, such as you get from looking down on the roof of a house. The height is a threshold from which to step down into the wooded folds of the land, the interior, under the trees and along the branching streams.

I pass through a pasture gate on a deep-worn path that grows shallow a little way beyond, and then disappears altogether into the grass. The gate has gathered thousands of passings to and fro that have divided like the slats of a fan on either side of it. It is like a fist holding together the strands of a net.

Beyond the gate the land leans always more steeply toward the branch. I follow it down, and then bear left along the crease at the bottom of the slope. I have entered the downflow of the land. The way I am going is the way the water goes. There is something comfortable and fit-feeling in this, something free in this yielding to gravity and taking the shortest way down.

As the hollow deepens into the hill, before it has yet entered the woods, the grassy crease becomes a raw gully, and along the steepening slopes on either side I can see the old scars of erosion, places where the earth is gone clear to the rock. My people's errors have become the features of my country.

It occurs to me that it is no longer possible to imagine how this country looked in the beginning, before the white people drove their plows into it. It is not possible to know what was the shape of the land here in this hollow when it was first cleared. Too much of it is gone, loosened by the plows and washed away by the rain. I am walking the route of the departure of the virgin soil of the hill. I am not looking at the same land the firstcomers saw. The original surface of the hill is as extinct as the passenger pigeon. The pristine America that the first white man saw is a lost continent, sunk like Atlantis in the sea. The thought of what was here once and is gone forever will not leave me as long as I live. It is as though I walk knee-deep in its absence.

The slopes along the hollow steepen still more, and I go in under the trees. I pass beneath the surface. I am enclosed, and my sense, my interior sense, of the country becomes intricate. There is no longer the possibility of seeing very far. The distances are closed off by the trees and the steepening walls of the hollow. One cannot grow familiar here by sitting and looking as one can up in the open on the ridge. Here the eyes become dependent on the feet. To see the woods from the inside one must look and move and look again. It is inexhaustible in its standpoints.

Wherever one goes along the streams of this part of the country, one is apt to come upon old stonework. There are walled springs and pools. There are the walls built in the steeper hollows where the fences cross or used to cross; the streams have drifted dirt in behind them, so that now where they are still intact they make waterfalls that have scooped out small pools at their feet. And there used to be miles of stone fences, now mostly scattered and sifted back into the ground.

Considering these, one senses a historical patience, now also extinct in the country. These walls were built by men working long days for little wages, or by slaves. It was work that could not be hurried at, a meticulous finding and fitting together, as though reconstructing a previous wall that had been broken up and scattered like puzzle pieces. The wall would advance only a few yards a day. The pace of it could not be borne by most modern men, even if the wages could be afforded. Those men had to move in closer accord with their own rhythms, and nature's, than we do. They had no machines. Their capacities were only those of flesh and blood. They talked as they worked. They joked and laughed. They sang. The work was exacting and heavy and hard and slow. No opportunity for pleasure was missed or slighted. The days and the years were long. The work was long. At the end of this job the next would begin. Therefore, be patient. Such pleasure as there is, is here, now. Take pleasure as it comes. Take work as it comes. The end may never come, or when it does it may be the wrong end.

Now the men who built the walls and the men who had them built have long gone underground to be, along with the buried ledges and the roots and the burrowing animals, a part of the nature of the place in the minds of the ones who come after them. I think of them lying still in their graves, as level as the sills and thresholds of their lives, as though resisting to the last the slant of the ground. And their old walls, too, re-enter nature, collecting lichens and mosses with patience their builders never conceived.

I have already passed the place where water began to flow in the little stream bed I am following. It broke into the light from beneath a rock ledge, a thin glittering stream. It lies beside me as I walk, overtaking me and going by, yet not moving, a thread of light and sound. And now from below comes the steady tumble and rush of the water of Camp Branch—whose nameless camp was it named for?—and gradually as I descend the sound of the smaller stream is lost in the sound of the larger.

The two hollows join, the line of the meeting of the two spaces obscured even in winter by the trees. But the two streams meet precisely as two roads. That is, the stream *beds* do; the one ends in the other. As for the meeting of the waters, there is no looking at that. The one flow does not end in the other, but continues in it, one with it, two clarities merged without a shadow.

All waters are one. This is a reach of the sea, flung like a net over the hill, and now drawn back to the sea. And as the sea is never raised in the earthly nets of fishermen, so the hill is never caught and pulled down by the watery net of the sea. But always a little of it is. Each of the gathering strands of the net carries back some of the hill melted in it. Sometimes, as now, it carries so little that the water flows clear; sometimes it carries a lot and is brown and heavy with it. Whenever greedy or thoughtless men have lived on it, the hill has literally flowed out of their tracks into the bottom of the sea.

There appears to be a law that when creatures have reached the level of consciousness, as men have, they must become conscious of the creation; they must learn how they fit into it and what its needs are and what it requires of them, or else pay a terrible penalty: the spirit of the creation will go out of them, and they will become destructive; the very earth will depart from them and go where they cannot follow.

My mind is never empty or idle at the joinings of streams. Here is the work of the world going on. The creation is felt, alive and intent on its materials, in such places. In the angle of the meeting of the two streams stands the steep wooded point of the ridge, like the prow of an upturned boat—finished, as it was a thousand years ago, as it will be in a thousand years. Its becoming is only incidental to its being. It will be because it is. It has no aim or end except to be. By being, it is growing and wearing into what it will be. The fork of the stream lies at the foot of the slope like hammer and chisel laid down at the foot of a finished sculpture. But the stream is no dead tool; it is alive, it is still at its work. Put your hand to it to learn the health of this part of the world. It is the wrist of the hill.

Perhaps it is to prepare to hear some day the music of the spheres that I am always turning my ears to the music of streams. There is indeed a music in streams, but it is not for the hurried. It has to be loitered by and imagined. Or imagined *toward*, for it is hardly for men at all. Nature has a patient ear. To her the slowest funeral march sounds like a jig. She is satisfied to have the notes drawn out to the lengths of days or weeks or months. Small variations are acceptable to her, modulations as leisurely as the opening of a flower.

The stream is full of stops and gates. Here it has piled up rocks in its path, and pours over them into a tiny pool it has scooped at the foot of its fall. Here it has been dammed by a mat of leaves caught behind a fallen limb. Here it must force a narrow passage, here a wider one. Tomorrow the flow may increase or slacken, and the tone will shift. In an hour or a week that rock may give way, and the composition will advance by another note. Some idea of it may be got by walking slowly along and noting the changes as one passes from one little fall or rapid to another. But this is a highly simplified and diluted version

of the real thing, which is too complex and widespread ever to be actually heard by us. The ear must imagine an impossible patience in order to grasp even the unimaginableness of such music.

But the creation is musical, and this is a part of its music, as bird song is, or the words of poets. The music of the streams is the music of the shaping of the earth, by which the rocks are pushed and shifted downward toward the level of the sea.

And now I find an empty beer can lying in the path. This is the track of the ubiquitous man Friday of all our woods. In my walks I never fail to discover some sign that he has preceded me. I find his empty shotgun shells, his empty cans and bottles, his sandwich wrappings. In wooded places along roadsides one is apt to find, as well, his overtraveled bedsprings, his outcast refrigerator, and heaps of the imperishable refuse of his modern kitchen. A year ago, almost in this same place where I have found his beer can, I found a possum that he had shot dead and left lying, in celebration of his manhood. He is the true American pioneer, perfectly at rest in his assumption that he is the first and the last whose inheritance and fate this place will ever be. Going forth, as he may think, to sow, he only broadcasts his effects.

I stoop between the strands of a barbed-wire fence, and in that movement I go out of time into timelessness. I come into a wild place. The trees grow big, their trunks rising clean, free of undergrowth. The place has a serenity and dignity that one feels immediately; the creation is whole in it and unobstructed. It is free of the strivings and dissatisfactions, the partialities and imperfections of places under the mechanical dominance of men. Here, what to a housekeeper's eye might seem disorderly is nonetheless orderly and within order; what might seem arbitrary or accidental is included in the design of the whole; what might seem evil or violent is a comfortable member of the household. Where the creation is whole nothing is extraneous. The presence of the creation here makes this a holy place, and it is as a pilgrim that I have come. It is the creation that has attracted me, its perfect interfusion of life and design. I have made myself its follower and its apprentice.

One early morning last spring, I came and found the woods floor strewn with bluebells. In the cool sunlight and the lacy shadows of the spring woods the blueness of those flowers, their elegant shape, their delicate fresh scent kept me standing and looking. I found a delight in them that I cannot describe and that I will never forget. Though I had been familiar for years with most of the spring woods flowers, I had never seen these and had not known they were here. Looking at them, I felt a strange loss and sorrow that I had never seen them before. But I was also exultant that I saw them now — that they were here.

For me, in the thought of them will always be the sense of the joyful surprise with which I found them — the sense that came suddenly to me then that the world is blessed beyond my understanding, more abundantly than I will ever know. What lives are still ahead of me here to be discovered and exulted in, tomorrow, or in twenty years? What wonder will be found here on the morning after my death? Though as a man I inherit great evils and the possibility of great loss and suffering, I know that my life is blessed and graced by the yearly flowering of the bluebells. How perfect they are! In their presence I am humble and joyful. If I were given all the learning and all the methods of my race I could not make one of them, or even imagine one. Solomon in all his glory was not arrayed like one of these. It is the privilege and the labor of the apprentice of creation to come with his imagination into the unimaginable, and with his speech into the unspeakable.

SECTION TWO

Traveling at Home

Even in a country you know by heart
it's hard to go the same way twice.
The life of the going changes.
The chances change and make a new way.
Any tree or stone or bird
can be the bud of a new direction. The
natural correction is to make intent
of accident. To get back before dark
is the art of going.

The Winter Rain

The leveling of the water, its increase,
the gathering of many into much:

in the cold dusk I stop
midway of the creek, listening
as it passes downward
loud over the rocks, under
the sound of the rain striking,
nowhere any sound
but the water, the dead
weedstems soaked with it, the
ground soaked, the earth overflowing.

And having waded all the way
across, I look back and see there
on the water the still sky.

Winter Night Poem for Mary

As I started home after dark
I looked into the sky and saw the new moon,
an old man with a basket on his arm.
He walked among the cedars in the bare woods.
They stood like guardians, dark
as he passed. He might have been singing,
or he might not. He might have been sowing
the spring flowers, or he might not. But I saw him
with his basket, going along the hilltop.

Meditation in the Spring Rain

In the April rain I climbed up to drink
of the live water leaping off the hill,
white over the rocks. Where the mossy root
of a sycamore cups the flow, I drank
and saw the branches feathered with green.
The thickets, I said, send up their praise
at dawn. Was that what I meant—I meant
my words to have the heft and grace, the flight
and weight of the very hill, its life
rising—or was it some old exultation
that abides with me? We'll not soon escape
the faith of our fathers—no more than
crazy old Mrs Gaines, whom my grandmother
remembers standing balanced eighty years ago
atop a fence in Port Royal, Kentucky,
singing: "One Lord, one Faith, and one
Cornbread." They had a cage built for her
in a room, "nearly as big as the room, not
cramped up," and when she grew wild
they kept her there. But mostly she went free
in the town, and they allowed the children
to go for walks with her. She strayed once
beyond where they thought she went, was lost
to them, "and they had an awful time
finding her." For her, to be free

was only to be lost. What is it about her
that draws me on, so that my mind becomes a child
to follow after her? An old woman
when my grandmother was a girl, she must have seen
the virgin forest standing here, the amplitude
of our beginning, of which no speech
remains. Out of the town's lost history,
buried in minds long buried, she has come,
brought back by a memory near death. I see her
in her dusky clothes, hair uncombed, the children
following. I see her wandering, muttering
to herself as her way was, among these hills
half a century before my birth, in the silence
of such speech as I know. Dawn and twilight
and dawn again trembling in the leaves
over her, she tramped the raveling verges
of her time. It was a shadowy country
that she knew, holding a darkness that was past
and a darkness to come. The fleeting lights
tattered her churchly speech to mad song.
When her poor wandering head broke the confines
of all any of them knew, they put her in a cage.
But I am glad to know it was a commodious cage,
not cramped up. And I am glad to know
that other times the town left her free
to be as she was in it, and to go her way.
May it abide a poet with as much grace!
For I too am perhaps a little mad,

standing here wet in the drizzle, listening
to the clashing syllables of the water. Surely
there is a great Word being put together here.
I begin to hear it gather in the opening
of the flowers and the leafing-out of the trees,
in the growth of bird nests in the crotches
of the branches, in the settling of the dead
leaves into the ground, in the whittling
of beetle and grub, in my thoughts
moving in the hill's flesh. Coming here,
I crossed a place where a stream flows
underground, and the sounds of the hidden water
and the water come to light braided in my ear.
I think the maker is here, creating his hill
as it will be, out of what it was.
The thickets, I say, send up their praise
at dawn! One Lord, one Faith, and one Cornbread
forever! But hush. Wait. Be as still
as the dead and the unborn in whose silence
that old one walked, muttering and singing,
followed by the children.

                 For a time there
I turned away from the words I knew, and was lost.
For a time I was lost and free, speechless
in the multitudinous assembling of his Word.

History

for Wallace Stegner

I.

The crops were made, the leaves
were down, three frosts had lain
upon the broad stone
step beneath the door;
as I walked away
the houses were shut, quiet
under their drifting smokes,
the women stooped at the hearths.
Beyond the farthest tracks
of any domestic beast
my way led me, into
a place for which I knew
no names. I went by paths
that bespoke intelligence
and memory I did not know.
Noonday held sounds of moving
water, moving air, enormous
stillness of old trees.
Though I was weary and alone,
song was near me then,
wordless and gay as a deer
lightly stepping. Learning
the landmarks and the ways
of that land, so I might
go back, if I wanted to,

my mind grew new, and lost
the backward way. I stood
at last, long hunter and child,
where this valley opened,
a word I seemed to know
though I had not heard it.
Behind me, along the crooks
and slants of my approach,
a low song sang itself,
as patient as the light.
On the valley floor the woods
grew rich: great poplars,
beeches, sycamores,
walnuts, sweet gums, lindens,
oaks. They stood apart
and open, the winter light
at rest among them. Yes,
and as I came down
I heard a little stream
pouring into the river.

2.
Since then I have arrived here
many times. I have come
on foot, on horseback, by boat,
and by machine—by earth,
water, air, and fire.
I came with axe and rifle.

I came with a sharp eye
and the price of land. I came
in bondage, and I came
in freedom not worth the name.
From the high outlook
of that first day I have come
down two hundred years
across the worked and wasted
slopes, by eroding tracks
of the joyless horsepower of greed.
Through my history's despite
and ruin, I have come
to its remainder, and here
have made the beginning
of a farm intended to become
my art of being here.
By it I would instruct
my wants: they should belong

to each other and to this place.
Until my song comes here
to learn its words, my art
is but the hope of song.

3.
All the lives this place
has had, I have. I eat
my history day by day.
Bird, butterfly, and flower
pass through the seasons of
my flesh. I dine and thrive
on offal and old stone,
and am combined within
the story of the ground.
By this earth's life, I have
its greed and innocence,
its violence, its peace.
Now let me feed my song
upon the life that is here
that is the life that is gone.
This blood has turned to dust
and liquefied again in stem
and vein ten thousand times.
Let what is in the flesh,
O Muse, be brought to mind.

Woods

I part the out thrusting branches
and come in beneath
the blessed and the blessing trees.
Though I am silent
there is singing around me.
Though I am dark
there is vision around me.
Though I am heavy
there is flight around me.

The Lilies

Hunting them, a man must sweat, bear
the whine of a mosquito in his ear,
grow thirsty, tired, despair perhaps
of ever finding them, walk a long way.
He must give himself over to chance,
for they live beyond prediction.
He must give himself over to patience,
for they live beyond will. He must be led
along the hill as by a prayer.
If he finds them anywhere, he will find
a few, paired on their stalks,
at ease in the air as souls in bliss.
I found them here at first without hunting,
by grace, as all beauties are first found.
I have hunted and not found them here.
Found, unfound, they breathe their light
into the mind, year after year.

Another Descent

Through the weeks of deep snow
we walked above the ground
on fallen sky, as though we did
not come of root and leaf, as though
we had only air and weather
for our difficult home.
                              But now
as March warms, and the rivulets
run like birdsong on the slopes,
and the branches of light sing in the hills,
slowly we return to earth.

Creation Myth

This is a story handed down.
It is about the old days when Bill
and Florence and a lot of their kin
lived in the little tin-roofed house
beside the woods, below the hill.
Mornings, they went up the hill
to work, Florence to the house,
the men and boys to the field.
Evenings, they all came home again.
There would be talk then and laughter
and taking of ease around the porch
while the summer night closed.
But one night, McKinley, Bill's younger brother,
stayed away late, and it was dark

when he started down the hill.
Not a star shone, not a window.
What he was going down into was
the dark, only his footsteps sounding
to prove he trod the ground. And Bill
who had got up to cool himself,
thinking and smoking, leaning on
the jamb of the open front door,
heard McKinley coming down,
and heard his steps beat faster
as he came, for McKinley felt the pasture's
darkness joined to all the rest
of darkness everywhere. It touched
the depths of woods and sky and grave.
In that huge dark, things that usually
stayed put might get around, as fish
in pond or slue get loose in flood.
Oh, things could be coming close
that never had come close before.
He missed the house and went on down
and crossed the draw and pounded on
where the pasture widened on the other side,
lost then for sure. Propped in the door,
Bill heard him circling, a dark star
in the dark, breathing hard, his feet
blind on the little reality
that was left. Amused, Bill smoked
his smoke, and listened. He knew where

McKinley was, though McKinley didn't.
Bill smiled in the darkness to himself,
and let McKinley run until his steps
approached something really to fear:
the quarry pool. Bill quit his pipe
then, opened the screen, and stepped out,
barefoot, on the warm boards. "McKinley!"
he said, and laid the field out clear
under McKinley's feet, and placed
the map of it in his head.

In Rain

1.

I go in under foliage
light with rain-light
in the hill's cleft,
and climb, my steps
silent as flight
on the wet leaves.
Where I go, stones
are wearing away
under the sky's flow.

2.

The path I follow
I can hardly see
it is so faintly trod
and overgrown.
At times, looking,
I fail to find it
among dark trunks, leaves
living and dead. And then
I am alone, the woods
shapeless around me.
I look away, my gaze
at rest among leaves,
and then I see the path

again, a dark way going on
through the light.

3.
In a mist of light
falling with the rain
I walk this ground
of which dead men
and women I have loved
are part, as they
are part of me. In earth,
in blood, in mind,
the dead and living
into each other pass,
as the living pass
in and out of loves
as stepping to a song.
The way I go is
marriage to this place,
grace beyond chance,
love's braided dance
covering the world.

4.
Marriages to marriages
are joined, husband and wife
are plighted to all
husbands and wives,

any life has all lives
for its delight.
Let the rain come,
the sun, and then the dark,
for I will rest
in an easy bed tonight.

SECTION THREE

The Bell Calls in the Town

The bell calls in the town
Where forebears cleared the shaded land
And brought high daylight down
To shine on field and trodden road.
I hear, but understand
Contrarily, and walk into the woods.
I leave labor and load,
Take up a different story.
I keep an inventory
Of wonders and of uncommercial goods.

I climb up through the field
That my long labor has kept clear.
Projects, plans unfulfilled
Waylay and snatch at me like briars,
For there is no rest here

43

Where ceaseless effort seems to be required,
Yet fails, and spirit tires
With flesh, because failure
And weariness are sure
In all that mortal wishing has inspired.

I go in pilgrimage
Across an old fenced boundary
To wildness without age
Where, in their long dominion,
The trees have been left free.
They call the soil here "Eden"; slants and steeps
Hard to stand straight upon
Even without a burden.
No more a perfect garden,
There's an immortal memory that it keeps.

I leave work's daily rule
And come here to this restful place
Where music stirs the pool
And from high stations of the air
Fall notes of wordless grace,
Strewn remnants of the primal Sabbath's hymn.
And I remember here
A tale of evil twined
With good, serpent and vine,
And innocence as evil's strategem.

I let that go a while,
For it is hopeless to correct
By generations' toil,
And I let go my hopes and plans
That no toil can perfect.
There is no vision here but what is seen:
White bloom nothing explains
But a mute blessedness
Exceeding all distress,
The fresh light stained a hundred shades of green.

Uproar of wheel and fire
That has contained us like a cell
Opens and lets us hear
A stillness longer than all time
Where leaf and song fulfill
The passing light, pass with the light, return,

Renewed, as in a rhyme.
This is no human vision
Subject to our revision;
God's eye holds every leaf as light is worn.

Ruin is in place here:
The dead leaves rotting on the ground,
The live leaves in the air
Are gathered in a single dance
That turns them round and round.
The fox cub trots his almost pathless path
As silent as his absence.
These passings resurrect
A joy without defect,
The life that steps and sings in ways of death.

The Eager Dog Lies Strange and Still

The eager dog lies strange and still
Who roamed the woods with me;
Then while I stood or climbed the hill
Or sat under a tree,

Awaiting what more time might say,
He thrashed in undergrowth,
Pursuing what he scared away,
Made ruckus for us both.

He's dead; I go more quiet now,
Stillness added to me
By time and sorrow, mortal law,
By loss of company

That his new absence has made new.
Though it must come by doom,
This quiet comes by kindness too,
And brings me nearer home,

For as I walk the wooded land
The morning of God's mercy,
Beyond the work of mortal hand,
Seen by more than I see,

The quiet deer look up and wait,
Held still in quick of grace.
And I wait, stop footstep and thought.
We stand here face to face.

Thrush Song, Stream Song, Holy Love

Thrush song, stream song, holy love
That flows through earthly forms and folds,
The song of Heaven's Sabbath fleshed
In throat and ear, in stream and stone,
A grace living here as we live,
Move my mind now to that which holds
Things as they change.
                              The warmth has come.
The doors have opened. Flower and song
Embroider ground and air, lead me
Beside the healing field that waits;
Growth, death, and a restoring form
Of human use will make it well.
But I go on, beyond, higher
In the hill's fold, forget the time
I come from and go to, recall

49

This grove left out of all account,
A place enclosed in song.
                              Design
Now falls from thought. I go amazed
Into the maze of a design
That mind can follow but not know,
Apparent, plain, and yet unknown,
The outline lost in earth and sky.
What form wakens and rumples this?
Be still. A man who seems to be
A gardener rises out of the ground,
Stands like a tree, shakes off the dark,
The bluebells opening at his feet,
The light one figured cloth of song.

The Year Relents

The year relents, and free
Of work, I climb again
To where the old trees wait,
Time out of mind. I hear
Traffic down on the road,
Engines high overhead.
And then a quiet comes,
A cleft in time, silence
Of metal moved by fire;
The air holds little voices,
Titmice and chickadees,
Feeding through the treetops
Among the new small leaves,
Calling again to mind
The grace of circumstance,
Sabbath economy
In which all thought is song,
All labor is a dance.
The world is made at rest,
In ease of gravity.
I hear the ancient theme
In low world-shaping song
Sung by the falling stream.
Here where a rotting log
Has slowed the flow: a shelf

Of dark soil, level laid
Above the tumbled stone.
Roots fasten it in place.
It will be here a while;
What holds it here decays.
A richness from above,
Brought down, is held, and holds
A little while in flow.
Stem and leaf grow from it.
At cost of death, it has
A life. Thus falling founds,
Unmaking makes the world.

A Tired Man Leaves His Labor

A tired man leaves his labor, felt
In every ligament, to walk
Alone across the new-mowed field,
And at its bound, the last cut stalk,

He takes a road much overgone
In time by bearers of his name,
Though now where foot and hoof beat stone
And passed to what their toil became,

Trees stand that in their long leaf-fall,
Untroubled on forgiving ground,
Have buried the sledged stone with soil
So that his passing makes no sound.

He turns aside, and joins his quiet
Forbears in absence from that way.
He passes through the dappled light
And shadow that the breeze makes sway

Upon him and around him as
He goes. Within the day's design
The leaves sway, darkly, or ablaze
Around their edges with a line

Of fire caught from the sun. He steps
Amid a foliage of song
No tone of which has passed his lips.
Watching, silent, he shifts among

The shiftings of the day, himself
A shifting of the day's design
Whose outline is in doubt, unsafe,
And dark. One time, less learned in pain,

He thought the earth was firm, his own,
But now he knows that all not raised
By fire, by water is brought down.
The slope his fields lie on is poised

Above the river in mere air,
The breaking forewall of a wave,
And everything he has made there
Floats lightly on that fall. To save

What passes is a passing hope
Within the day's design outlawed.
His passing now has brought him up
Into a place not reached by road,

Beyond all history that he knows,
Where trees like great saints stand in time,

Eternal in their patience. Loss
Has rectified the songs that come

Into this columned room, and he
Only in silence, nothing in hand,
Comes here. A generosity
Is here by which the fallen stand.

In history many-named, in time
Nameless, this amplitude conveys
The answering to the asking rhyme
Among confusions that dispraise

The membering name that Adam spoke
By gift, and then heard parcelled out
Among all fallen things that croak
And cry and sing and curse and shout.

The foliage opens like a cloud.
At rest high on the valley side,
Silent, the man looks at the loud
World: road and farm, his daily bread,

His beasts, his garden, and his barns,
His trees, the white walls of his house,
Whose lives and hopes he knows. He yearns
Toward all his work has joined. What has

He by his making made but home,
A present help by passing grace
Allowed to creatures of his name
Here in this passing time and place?

Wendell Berry lives on the Kentucky River near the town of Port Royal. A farmer, poet, essayist, professor, and novelist, Berry has published four novels, a book of short stories, ten of poetry, and nine of essays. Recently he received an award from the American Academy and Institute of Arts and Letters.